LIVE CANON
2018 Children's Anthology

First Published in 2018
By Live Canon Ltd
www.livecanon.co.uk

978-1-909703-30-8

A CIP catalogue record for this book is available from the British Library.

The poems in this anthology were shortlisted for the 2018 Live Canon Poetry Competition for young writers aged 5 to 18

Contents

Superhero Me
Jedidiah Wale-Akinlua

There is a superhero that is me
I want to fly across the whole world
I want to have laser eyes so that I can shoot out lasers
It would be amazing to have laser eyes
I want to see through people
To know what they are thinking
To tell their minds and make them laugh
To say their thoughts and make them smile
Nothing would be cooler than that.
To be a superhero
Just nothing!!!

Freedom
Ryder Purcell

Freedom is a
Tarantula hunting quietly
Tiger stalking carefully
Dinosaur roaring loudly

All About Myself

Zoë Moore

Naughty knotty hair
Brown like a hedgehog

Lovely lightish freckles
Scattered around my face

My eyes are blue like waves
They twinkle when I'm cheeky

Silly like a clown,
I like dolphins and turtles

Gymnastics is my favourite
Monkeying on the bars

I try my best to not
Be mean
And to make my handwriting neat

Five years old
(but nearly six)
April eighteenth
Is the day of my birth

Shoreham is my home
I take pride in it

My life is sometimes easy
And sometimes hard
But I laugh all the time
I am really crazy

My Family

Alma Bhim

by Alma Bhim

My family

When I was zaro, I opend my eyes and thoght
the wold was amaizg.
I didont know everybody but they knew me
I felt happy when they felt happy and I still do.
My family are far from me and close to me and just
around the corner.
They are from all diffrent colours of the rainbow.
They are all special and make me special.
Now I am seven and I know my family better and better.
family FAMILy family FAMILy

What if the Underground had Transport for Rabbits and Woodlice?

Emily Ramen-Christensen

What if the underground had transport for rabbits and woodlice?
They would have their own little seats
And blankets for their laps
And small pieces of wood to eat

The rabbit conductor would say mind the gap because it is big
The other rabbits would burrow tunnels for the tubes to whoosh through
Paws digging, nose twitching and whiskers wriggling
The will be no escalators just a helter skelter

2 million woodlice traveling to work
Good morning… Good morning… And yawning to you
We are off to work, can you come too?

The sky is dark, hey we like it like that
We live in the woods, we live in burrows
You London commuters work on computers

Our underground world is simple and full of nature
Not like your stations full of no nature
Don't take a look as you will disturb
We are happy in our underground world

Snowflake

George Cook

Snow as soft as silky feathers from such a giant bird
Nearby chattering children can be heard
Observing snowflakes falling from the sky
Whirling snowflakes from up high
Fantastic falling flakes of snow
Levitating very slow
All of the ground is covered in white
Keeping the ground looking like clouds
Each snowflake has a pointy edge

What Can You See?

Ishaan Godber

What can you see? What can you see?
I can see a cute robin flying away from me.
Little robin, little robin, what can you see?
I can see Ishaan looking at me.
Ishaan, Ishaan what can you see?
I can see a beautiful butterfly flying to a tree.
Butterfly, butterfly, what can you see?
I can see a bird flying making me dizzy.
Birdie, birdie, what can you see?
I can see a worm that looks very tasty.
Worm, worm, what can you see?
I can see a caterpillar eating a blackberry.
Caterpillar, caterpillar, what can you see?
I can see a butterfly, I wish that was ME!

A Bird's Life

Pererin Harper

High up in the trees
Tweeting sweet songs...

Down upon the ground
A little dog appears, and barks.

They carry on their sweet song
Making their nests with their young.

They raise them well, with food and shelter -
Then they learn to fly.
But then it's time to fly away
Find another place to stay
And that's the end.

Walrus

Rishan Mistry

Walrus, Walrus what is your name?
Never mind, I am going to call you Paint,
Because when you are in the sun,
The sun paints you red.
Paint, Paint, your name is Paint.

You are amazing,
Because you can sleep when you are swimming.
You swim like a fish,
You can swim faster than a bear.

You have thick skin to keep you warm in the cool sea,
To protect you from polar bears, who we don't see.
Walrus, Walrus what is your game?

Flowers Grow
Rosa Lambert

Flowers grow
From head to toe
Not fast, but slow.

Flowers grow
Then they are picked
And put into a vase.

When they die
They droop their heads.
But soon new flowers grow
And you know how
Because I told you so.

Did you guess it too?
Amelia Atcheson

Munching thriller
not a killer not a
gorilla no,
thanks!

Might be a penguin might be a fish
might be a seal but that's not it!

Could be a monkey
could be a lion he's a
very hairy fella' and a
good climber too.

He's a squirrel!
Did you guess it too?

The Dust of Rhyme

Isabel Kinchen

Do you see the sparks
Do you think they're fairies?
Or are they memories.
Older older, taller taller
That's time, but the spark
Is the dust of rhyme
Do you feel the rhythm in your feet?
Just dance and you'll be better
Darling they are angels in the sky
Older and older, taller and taller
That's time, but the sparks
Are the dust of rhyme

I Am a Snowflake

Isobel Adie

I am a snowflake
I look down at the ground
I quiver and quake
at London's noise and sound.

I feel winter's cold breeze
as it lifts me into the air
I look down at the trees
I stare, and stare, and stare.

It's been a real treat,
but now I'm down
it's bittersweet
my face is wearing a frown.

I'm now some snow
under your feet, down below.

Seasons

James Fisher

Spring

Day is the same length as night
And it's getting very bright.
And all the rain in April brings
Daffodils and other things.
Daisies come up from the ground
And the great tit's call does sound.

Summer

Sun, flowers,
Fun for hours.

Autumn

Orange-yellow trees
Shaken by the breeze.
Leaves are falling fast;
Winter's come at last.

Winter

Frost, snow and ice
All as white as rice.
Trees without leaves,
Everything will freeze.

Volcano

Kayah Jalowiec

Lava cracking through the black veil,
Magma making its betrayal
BANG! LAVA! CRASH!
Boulders falling in a flash,
Make it snappy
Don't interrupt,
When volcanos blow,
They do erupt

Lava fragments as big as grenades,
Ruining all the Java parades
It's got way too much on its plate,
Or is my rescue just too late
Will this be everlasting violence,
BOOM! CRASH!
Then there's silence

It's Winter Here

Peggy Strachan

It's winter here in Scotland and I'm about to light my fire.
I'm freezing from head to toe.
I was freezing in bed.
I woke up in the morning and looked out at the snow, turned to my mum and said "It's awffy braw."
I went to school and had a blether and wished I could play forever and ever.

Tree

Lottie Caboche

Tree tree way up high in the sky
On a hill. No forest, no woods
Just a hill. A plain old hill.

Tree tree way up high in the sky
No-one no-one not even a single bird or mouse
No-one no-one no-one

Tree tree way up high in the sky
No heat no warmth
No fire not a single flame
Not a spark

Tree tree way up high in the sky
No-one comes to see this little tree
But suddenly
A girl a girl came and put something on him
Something red and round and BIG
"That tickles" thought tree

Tree tree way up high in the sky
Next day next day a group of people came
And put something long and blue and thin on him

Tree tree way up high in the sky
Next day a boy came
And put nine small round and orange things on him
And a yellow something on top

Tree tree way up high in the sky
Tree was happy now
Birds surrounded him
So he had friends

The Magic Box Poem

Neve Frances Macgregor

I will put in my box
A tree full of jeweled grapes
That taste of lemon curd.
Seagulls singing silent night,
The beautiful sense of the
Sun setting.

I will put in my box
A basket of tomatoes
A gentle humming singing
On the breeze
A rabbit with fur like silk

I will put in my box
A plate of never ending
Cookies. Some penguins
Playing rocking around the
Christmas tree on the piano
A shell made from gold
And silver.

I will put in my box
A basket of fat juicy oranges
Parrots chirruping the time
A never ending Christmas

My box is fashioned with
Glitter in the corners
And secrets in the lock
And wishes from far away
In the hinges

Autumn Poem

Phoenix Haddow

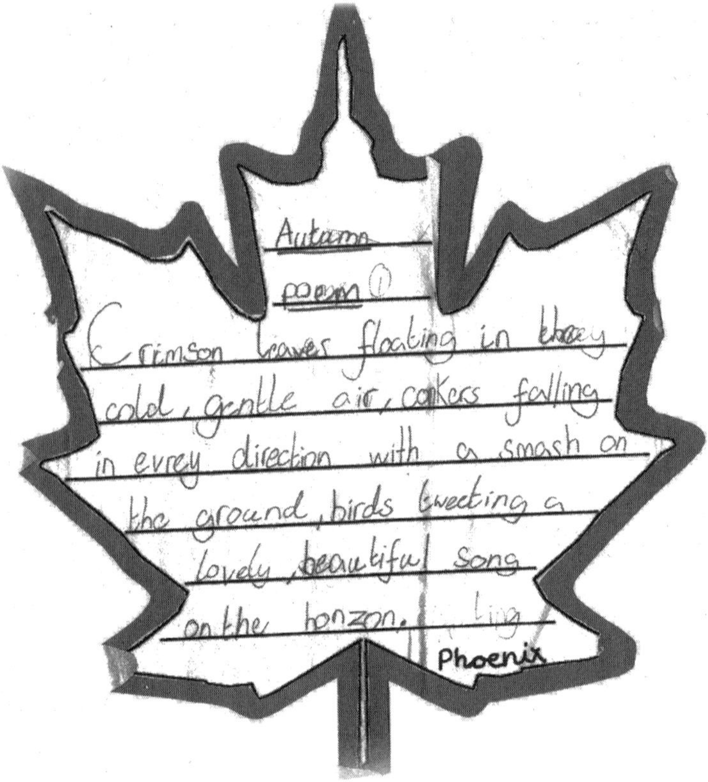

The Missing Words

Siena Violet Jones

One morning I woke up,
I couldn't hear the birds.
Everyone was so quiet,
Everything felt curved.

Everything was silent,
I couldn't hear the baby.
No one asked "can I have toast for lunch?",
And no one answered "maybe".

This is what had disappeared,
Nothing precious, something dear.
Everybody seemed so still –
Where are all the words to fill?

The tweeting of the birds,
The barking of the dog.
The blowing of the wind,
The squelching of a bog.

One morning I woke up,
I woke up very late.
No beeping of the alarm clock,
Maybe this was my fate.

The Sky's Tears
Alexandra McCaffery

The sky has its tantrums, like all of us,
The sky sometimes cries, like everyone must,
The sky sometimes shouts, in anger or glee,
The sky sometimes bellows, like you and like me,
The sky sometimes winces, in pain or in fear,
And whenever she does it, we'll always hear,
Sometimes tears roll down the sky's huge cheeks,
You think that she's lifeless, but really she speaks.

The Sky War
Ella McEwan

Rain is heaven's bombs dropping down on us cruelly
Sometimes though they bring messages of peace
Lightening is their gun shooting menacingly
Maybe hitting trees as fast as the speed of light

Great and white is the colour often shown in the clouds
Occasionally they are black like midnight diamonds
Thunder is their war song
Clapping loud as a lion's roar

Hailstones rain down like shooting bullets
They are made of guns of ice
Then the sun comes out burning us all
Like the last bomb hitting evilly

Finally, the rainbow comes out showing us all peace
We cheer hooray for we are free from the terrors of the Sky War

Meet the Family

Freya Lusty

My grandma Gabriella
Gets great giraffes
Gobbles gum
Greets gorillas
My grandma Gabriella is a gruesome granny.

My auntie Alex
Eats aqua apples
Argues with ants
Always arranges activities
My auntie Alex is an active auntie

My brother Bob
Bounces broccoli
Bakes bananas
Blows balloons
My brother Bob is a bouncy brother

My dad Dave
Dances disgracefully
Does dabs
Doesn't do washing
My dad Dave is a doing dad.

If I Had Sellotape

Freyja Crowder

If I had Sellotape I wouldn't get sticky hands
From my icity stickity glue

If I had Sellotape I would not be icity stickity
I would be extremely clean

I will never use glue
And that will be that!

But how will I stick my work down?
I did not think this through

I think I will stick with glue
Icity stickity glue

Our World

Leo Rees Smith

Wolves and sharks and singing larks,
Different realms they roam;
Padding paws, jagged jaws
And precious wings they own.

Bears on slopes and antelopes,
A ground squirrel the wolves seek.
Mountains high, eagles that fly,
Soaring up the tall peaks.

Fish and seal and the slimy eel,
In corals and trenches they swim.
Shallow to deep, flat to steep,
Bright light fades to dim.

Bushes and hedgerows and flowers that grow,
On roadsides and fields they bloom.
Towering trees, luscious leaves,
Creating scenes like a loom.

Trucks and cars and handle bars,
Busy roads they rule.
Lights are flashing, wheels are dashing,
Always burning fuel.

Sea and land and silky sand,
Covering the coastal shore.
Deep dark caves, crashing waves,
An almighty hypnotic roar.

Rain and snow and wind that blows,
The weather is always there.
Sun is shining, clouds are climbing
Freely through the air.

Nature and man should walk hand in hand,
So the planet's power is unfurled.
It's biodiverse, let's reverse man's curse
To protect Our Wonderful World.

My Pet is a Monster

Maisey Gubb

My pet is a monster
A treacherous ugly lobster

I found this monster in a tree
A Guinea pig he used to be

Another day I cry because he is a horrid fly

When I dress up as a wizard
He turns into a lizard

When I am very quiet
He is a ginormous giant

He smells like fishes breath
I am close to death

He eats rotten greasy stuff
And he traps you in handcuffs

When I am asleep in bed
He bursts into bloody red

UH! OH! Now I have no pet
Thank goodness he's dead

Reading Under a Tree

Meera Batakurki

Out on the fields,
where I
play with
paper shields,
is a tree.

It stands
high and tall,
and leans
against a wall.

That's where I
read all day,
everything around me
just fades away.

Dreaming of adventures,
I travel around the
world and
come across miles away.

I go through the
woods and far away lands
whilst I'm reading a book
that sits in my hands!

Dawn to Dark

Stella Odysseos

Birds flapping, screeching,
Clocks ticking and tocking.
Cockerels cooing and crowing,
The morning breeze swooshes and swashes.

Trees rustle and whisper,
Fishes splish and splash.
The horses stomp and neigh,
The sun beams and booms.

But when the sun goes down,
The owls start cooing and hooting.
Hedgehogs rustle and waddle about,
Wolves yip and yowl running free.

Now the moon is up,
And everything is silent.
Sssh!   Sssh!
As hush descends,
It is the end of another day.

Behind the Scenes

Talal Razouk

From DC comics
to marvel screens,
have you ever wondered
what happens behind the scenes?
Having fussing and arguing
of what to do
to make things interesting
for me and you;
Spending money on
many trips and in shoes
to make their way
to the scene they choose.
The info you've heard before
have been found out
and kicked out of the door.
Lies are hated
and can never be true
and they always try
to mess with you.

The Magic Box

Caoimhe Burden

I will put into the box
the steam from a memory as fresh as a legendary lion,
the slippery surface from the scorching sun,
and a howling secret swirling around the universe waiting to be spilled.

I will put into that box
the crackle of a blazing fire boiling the dinner of an old sailor,
the whisper of an oak tree dancing in the shadows of the night,
and the popping of an angel biting into the moon.

My box is fashioned with moondust for the inside,
and dragon wings for the hinges,
and pennies for the rim.
I will float in my box through the stars of China
to the moons of Pluto,
landing softly on a bed full of pillows.

The Path

Chloe Owen

Running between a forest and a village
Is the ghost of a meandering path
That, in days long passed,
served the milkman
With his horse, cantering back
From a hard day's work;
Foxes that paced, preparing to catch
Their dinner, as the grand old owl
Whistled to his mate.

Now, of a summer evening - late - when the
Night air cools on the trout-ringed pools,
And the squirrels spring from
Tree to tree, the path is gone.
Brambles and grasses have covered it,
While all around factories grow and grow
Until the forest is no more.

But some say, when the moon is full,
You can hear the horse pounding
And the whistle of the milk man
And the grand old owl whistling.

The Eagle

Elsie Moore

Silky, white wings, where are you going?
Smooth, black talons, what's for breakfast?
Bright, yellow eyes, what are you looking for?
Proud, grey stomach, why so fluffy?
Long, slim feathers, how can you bear to lose them?
Orange, hooked beak, why do you fish?

I am going to fish dear child I am going to fish for cod,
I fish for this over rolling seas or a slowly mingling river.

For breakfast this morning dear child for breakfast this morning is haddock,
I catch with my talons and tear with my beak and am not afraid to get wet!

I am looking for dear child I am looking for a tree,
somewhere to rest my head somewhere for three!

I am so fluffy dear child I am so fluffy for warmth,
when winter comes and snow falls I have no fire for heat!
I can't bear to lose my feathers dear child I can't bear to lose them at all,
I'm molting like mad it's getting bad I just wish I could stick them back on!
I fish for food dear child I fish for food like crabs,
I rip them and tear them, for me it's like burger and chips!
For I am eagle, eagle am I,
and I would never give up the ability to fly!

Story Ingredients

Emma Balduini

Full stops,
Adjectives,
That's what you need,
A sprinkle of emotion plants a seed.
Characters,
Dilemmas,
A little of those,
Then we watch how our story grows.
Metaphor, adverbs,
And similes,
Begin to build a narrative tree.
Take some speech marks,
And add some names,
Give your characters love, fear and fame.
This is how you make your story complete,
Isn't it nice and isn't it neat?
Hard work and focus that is key,
To keep building your narrative tree,
Alliteration adds a little fun,
There your story is almost done.
Let it simmer,
Let it bubble,
Finish it too early,
And you're in trouble.
Don't rebel and rush your work,
You never know where a great novel will lurk.
I feel our time is nearly at an end,
Go, write a classic my friend!

Beware of Baba Yaga

(from a Russian folk tale)

Freya Leech

In a chicken house
In a land of snow
In a wood
Where nobody dares to go
Lived a creepy old woman
Through a creepy old gate
Through a creepy old door
Surrounded by hate.
She's a haggard old hag
With a green pointy hat
And a long green cape
And a talking cat.
She flies in the night
With her pestle and mortar
Creeping through houses
To steal somebody's daughter.
When dawn is a-coming
She goes back to her lair
To pick all the creatures
That are caught in her hair.
And from her nose drips
Disgusting green slime.
She slurps it all up
To pass the long time.
When the night is coming
Children, run home
For it's bad to be out
In the woods all alone.
It's hard to get out
When you're in her grip.
You have to be crafty
To give her the slip.
Take something magic
When you go to the wood.
To get her away

You have to be good.
And maybe, just maybe,
If you're stuck in the wood
Think of this poem
And try to be good.

Sprouts!

Isabella Coppola

Never will I eat a sprout
Not even on Christmas day
Never will I eat a sprout
No matter what you say

The repulsive taste in my mouth
I would spit it out and pout
Not until pigs fly and mice shout
Will I eat a sprout

Never will I eat a sprout
Not even if I'm feeling kind
And no one
Can change my mind!

Pokemon Poem

Helena Binnie

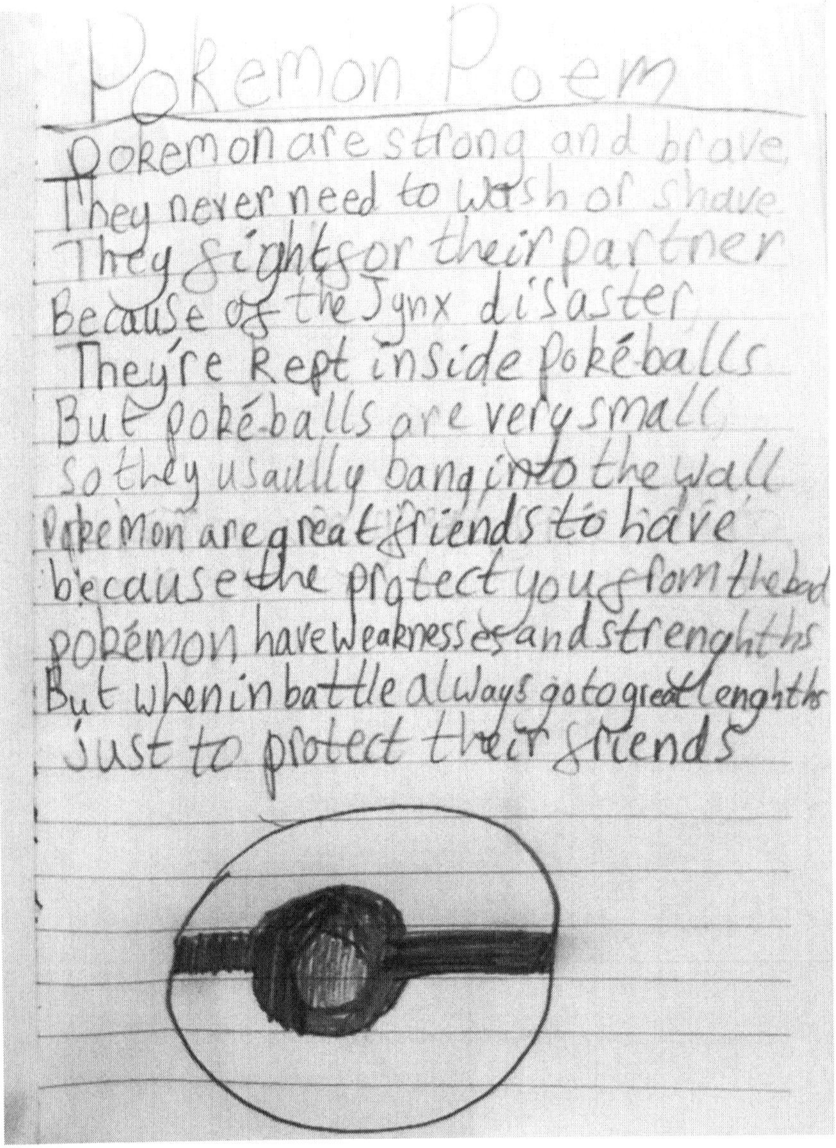

Pokemon Poem

Pokemon are strong and brave
They never need to wash or shave
They fights for their partner
Because of the Jynx disaster
They're kept inside poké-balls
But poké-balls are very small
So they usaully bang into the wall
Pokemon are great friends to have
because the protect you from the bad
pokémon have weaknesses and strenghths
But when in battle always go to great lenghths
just to protect their friends

Sleeptime

Lily Mellen-Daniel

In the fading, evening light,
It changes from day to night.
Squirrels, rabbits, weasels, all gone.
It's sleeptime, little one.

Stars emerge from behind the clouds,
It's all quiet now, not too loud.
Shhhh, shhhh, silence now…

The dark is a blanket
For the sun to lay on earth's bed,
So you can sleep peacefully,
Your dreams safe inside your head.

Pheasant in the Snow

Milo Hamilton-Raimondi

Snow had fallen in the night,
The lake was sparkling glass.
Trees were gently wrapped in white,
And sky was softest ash.

A beady eye, a blazing wing,
An emerald cap gleamed proudly.
A claret cape fit for a king
Sweeps over frozen carpet.

A glance, a strut, a nervous race,
A gallery of footprints.
A puzzled look, bespectacled face
Sights first snow of winter.

Snow had fallen in the night
And jewelled bird has taken flight

A Fish Life

Nicholas Skidmore

Fishes, fishes filling the sea
swimming silently.
Soaring through like lightning,
blowing your bubbles away
but you're very much prey.

As I Stand Here by the Ocean

Sarah Marine

As I stand here by the ocean
Breathing in the fresh air
The waves seem to motion to me
Flowing back all the memories of things that are now
Gone in the numerous years
The waves of overpowering thoughts
Like the whole ocean was in my mind
Jumbling all the loss and grief in my life
And into my head
I trying to push them away like normal
The water rippled through my body
As I thought about all the loss in my life
As I stand here by the ocean

The Fox's Star

Otto Hamilton-Raimondi

The night was cold. A swish of red
Through the silver forest fled.
Firs stood cloaked in powder white,
Majestic in the velvet night.

Eyes of magic wonder gleam,
As footprints race a glinting stream.
Tail a bushy, sweeping brush,
Swishes through the snowy hush.

Beyond the trees he leaps and seeks,
Ears are pointed russet peaks.
Then like a frosted statue, still.
Stands spellbound on the moonlit hill.

His gazing eyes wander far
And stop, upon a shining star.

Secret Life of Seasons

Rosa Kingcome

Lady Winter

Lady Winter glides over the frosty ground
Frozen leaves slowly drifting shaking hands
A silk white cloak made of frozen cobwebs draped over her shoulders
Crystallised snow quickly falling chatting together
She lives in the hollow of a pine tree
Bare trees quietly swaying crying for warmth
She sees mist hanging on strings
Her own breath not moving
She feels a pleasant wave rushing through her body made of crystals
Hard ground sitting quietly, begging to move
As she relaxes, she listens to the frosty paths gently swaying, singing a song of harmony.

Daughter of Spring

Nature stretching and yawning after its long refreshing sleep
The Daughter of Spring emerging from roots, beds of hay falling from her hair
What meets her eyes is a soothing sight
She sees red roses glistening like rubies
Fresh grass sparkling like emeralds
She sees butterflies, their wings dazzling white, soothing red or prickly brown
Beetles and bugs bustling past their grass made shops
With her head held high, she is proud of what her season holds.

Boy of Summer

Everyone thinks he's an ordinary boy but not quite, he is the boy of summer
He strides over clouds in the morning sun
He sings like a twittering bird
He nests in the treetops and prances in air
Yet he's solemn and means every word
He plays in the haystacks with all of his friends and his sister the daughter of spring
He means all well but is sometimes in hell
And that's his story to tell.

Sir Autumn

Sir Autumn skims the treetops like an eagle
He wears a robe made of rusty leaves, dripping silently like the tears of a tree
He sees his glistening breath dancing in air like sparks of magic
He feels the cool evening air streaming against his body
He listens to the ruby apples, cheeks red with laughter, playing in trees
A cradle of leaves waiting below.

Cardboard Box

Sophie Thomas

Card board box

It can be a boat,
though it can not float.

It can be a car,
travelling very far.

It can be a rocket,
taking off with a shocket.

It can be a hiding place,
though it does not have much space.

It can be anything you need,
As long as you take heed,
Of MAGNAION,
A child's play station.

So, go on, have a try!

By Sophie Thomas, 10   Illustrations by Kate Thomas, 10

The Nose Knows

Uma Buffong

Lavender's heavenly scent
Rotten eggs were never meant,
Blossom's fresh, springy smell,
Cold soggy sick, equals hell.
Roses' aroma brings you to heaven,
Old broccoli no-one likes, under seven.

Sweaty smells surround socks,
Odd smells lurk in nearby door locks,
Sweet smells lift you up to pure joy,
Flowery smells tiptoe, fragrant and coy,
Cheesy smells saunter, the stench is horrendous,
Baking bread smell always means tremendous,
The smell feet is a life ender,
But the smell of dog breath will make you surrender,
Perfumy smells are like a girly sister,
Medicine smells are like an annoying blister,
The sea's smell dances fresh and clear,
Pub's smells reek of beer,
The smell of hope is like a bright fresh field,
But the smell of love is happiness unpeeled.

Now you know hundreds of smells,
The ones we love and others worse than hell.
It's up to you to read again,
But if not I'm guessing it's
THE END

A Journey of Freedom

Yousif Ahmed Abdelaal-Wait

They carried me out into the moonlight,
Directly below the stars,
Placed me on a golden, glistening post,
And stroked me one last time.

I closed my eyes and silently prayed,
As I spread my healed wings out,
Looked up at the shining orb above,
Spilled one last tear over my plumage.

I flapped as hard as I could,
And fell into the light breeze,
As my wings took off
And I soared towards the stars above.

I flew over the forests,
And danced with the leaves,
As I tore up, up, up,
Through the moonlight I weaved.

Plummeted and swooped through footless halls of air,
Feeling the feeling of freedom,
I flit around the silent sanctity of space,
Where my tears plunged into the dark, blue ocean.

It began to rain,
Cold drops slipped through my feathers,
Winds drove me forwards,
Carrying me above the sparkling sea.

And come sun, blasting warmth through its rays,
Penetrating my body as I floated along the wind,
I flew with renewed energy, knowing my journey was not yet finished,
As the sun plunged into the sea and night's blackness rose again.

Many days and nights passed,
As I swooped above the sea,
Soon they turned into weeks,
And months of travelling I could see.

I flew among skyscrapers,
Lights shining below,
Busy cities passed beyond me,
As they waved a friendly hello.

I flew over the towering trees,
As freedom's adventure neared an end,
I tumbled down into the canopy,
Into my mother's soft, warm plumage.

Her love swept through my tired, aching feathers,
As freedom fluttered in my heart once again.
I chirped sweetly to myself under my breath,
Home…
Sweet…
Home.

Look and You'll See

Yuval Fransis

Under the trees
In a fairytale book
Above the clouds
In a giant's house
In a princess' castle
Or a birds nest
Who knows where magic will rest
Take a sneak peek
Maybe in wonderland
Perhaps you can see
That you're standing on it
Just look a little closer
And you will see
Magic is everywhere
Under your bed
Will you see a monster rest?
When you are sleeping
Do you see a fairy guard you?
Sniff a flower
Do you see magic there?
Under the dirt
Or up in a tree
It does not really matter
Nor should you care
Just look and you'll see
Magic is everywhere

Falling (based on Henry Matisse's *Jazz Icarus*)

Abigail Price

Silence.
The sun is pushing me down,
through the inky darkness.
No breath, no tears, no hope.
The deep sky without mercy,
letting me fall down, down towards my death.
I'm in shock; speechless and alone.
The stars are mocking me, filling my mind
With the sound of their cold laughter.
Screaming and crying inside, but nothing comes out.
My heart is beating so fast I can't hear it.
Faster and faster, pounding and thumping.
The last feather falls.
Silence.

Yonder

Archie Noyce

Soaring into the great sky above
Towards the shining sun far away
Until I'm as small as a dove
Upon the warm thermals of late May
The wind pushing my avian body high
Onwards I fly nearer to the sun
Enveloped in moist cloud and sky
Performing twists and having fun
Swerving through clouds' misty fog
Filling me with the purest of joy
Leaving me completely agog
The big blue space my toy
Making me cry out aloud
And turn around and spin
Voyaging through cloud after cloud
For I am the mighty peregrine.

Sheep's Skull

Frankie Vasseur

Horn like bubbly, frothing waves looming over the sea,
parched rotting bones snapping like trees,
rugged, ash teeth crumbling quicker and quicker,
a parted pathway leading to a garden of knowledge,
a devilish smile as it snaps and white snow falls.
Drips of silence. It turns night.

The Sea Cadet Cottage

Jessica Moffatt

As you enter the old musty building,
You hear creaking floorboards, screeching seagulls
And chattering sea cadets.
It makes you feel like you're at home.
You feel lively and happy.
A mix of extraordinary emotions,
As you touch the ancient walls, you spiral into a historic land.
The walls are rough of old age.
It really is a picturesque, white washed seaman's cottage,
And that's what makes it a special home for sea cadets.

Long Forgotten

Holly Tallulah Jones

The weight of the universe:
Drapes over my shoulders;
Streams behind me in a cascading lake of stars;
Distorts my body with its eternal unforgiveness;
Yet I get no appreciation.

I am creator of:
Death and life;
Suffering and torture;
Disease and sickness;
Failure and humiliation;
Hatred and misery;
Yet I get no objections.

I established:
Generosity and kindness;
Passion and love;
Loyalty and faith;
Delight and pleasure;
Yet I get no share of what miracles I have made.

I have experienced:
The unimaginable;
The unpredictable;
The unbearable;
The uninterested;
Yet I get no notice of my bravery.

I am drowned in:
Worry;
Anger;
Grief;
Sadness;
Danger;
Pain;
Yet I get no support.

I am Time, and I get nothing.
Why?
Because I have been long forgotten.
That I cannot change, despite my unfading existence.

The Path

Liam Baldry

Running through a valley,
A snow-coated dip
Between gorse-covered slopes,
There is a path. It winds
Between yellow-painted houses.
Ants crawl along the half-worn path
Over the muddy bank,
As the path winds
Like coiled plastic.
The children wear the valley,
Flattening the gorse.
Trees overhang it, and the
Path seems full of promises
But it ends when the wood ends.

Rundown Ruins

Lily-Mae Roísín Cooney

Twisted weeds conceal around the wicked wall,
Thirsty thistles detach their faded colours, desperate to drink,
Evil ivy slithers up the fractured remains that are ever so tall,
Thoughtless thorns sprout in the wilderness without one think!

Lifeless, abandoned nests are left stranded without care,
Nocturnal lairs lie unstabilised waiting for return,
Antique horse reins are neglected, with the odd trace of hair,
Eliminated pig sties are left helplessly camouflaged by fern!

Cottage debris is dispersed all over the non-surfaced lane,
A damaged chimney is upside down by the ghostly remains,
Aged curtains lie raggedly, by the traces of wreck, besides the ruins
in pain,
A shabby carpet covers the sooty floor, sheltering the packed drains!

The wonderful weather transforms with a blink,
Rich rain pours down, soaking the place from head to toe,
Whistling wind flies swiftly over the debris, blowing it with one
wink,
Sunshine sweeps the sky, conquering the rain, making rain the foe!

Broken heart,
Bone-like trees,
Walls apart,
No buzzing bees!

Cheetah

Oscar Hill

Running through the desert
Like a fire star,
With the burning sand
On my dark paws.
The crushed gold sparks up
From the flaring sand
As I shoot through the marathon desert,
Through the desolation.
The boiling spirits
In the sun,
Accusing the heat against me,
Draining my power and speed,
Making me vulnerable,
Drink all animals' power
To make themselves strong
Once again.
I have forgotten the taste of water,
Outlawed out of my mouth,
The breath of wind gone.
All I feel is the weakness
Of the dreadful heat
And the numbness of hunger.
I can not take one more leap.

Night avenges the sun.
Suddenly I feel regenerated
By glorious magic.
I make it to the other side,
Like a sibling learning its way
Through the harsh spirits of life,
The environment of the brain,
And the never-ending maze of sense.
Now I finally learn that I made it out alive.
The spirits have decided
They can not watch me die.
Shooting back my strength,

I slowly creep up
And I am reincarnated
Into a fresh strength.

Fog

Ted McKnight Hardy

The dead seedlings of mist
creep out of
the trees and into the distance

Sprinkling their magic over grass
as wind carries
across the landscape.

A rabbit skitters into
a burrow and
the fountain of shadows
join

Leaving vague silhouettes
of long lost trees and
the cut off breeze of
cold, grey
light.

Lady Macbeth's Madness

Rosabelle Jones

The blood of the king has stained my heart,
Left me with a smell which shall not part.
Although I already have my crown,
I cannot rid my face of this guilty frown.

For many months now I have lived in fear.
Yet never shedding a single tear.
For I see Duncan's body dead and still,
Forgetting why we chose to kill.

I retrace my steps, hanging my head,
Wishing I was still safe in bed.
The stench of death was an awful smell,
Yet now there is no one I can tell.

I escaped the corridor's blinding light,
I ran from the horrors of that night.
The demon of death clawed my brain,
As I walked the corridors of Dunsinane.

I run clutching my dead in despair,
Feeling the blood tangling my ruby red hair.
Guilt and regret make me feel like a fool,
For why would we commit a crime so cruel?

As I get nearer to the door,
I remember what life was like before:
The times when we had no throne,
The times when we were safe at home.

Yet Duncan is dead, the deed is done,
What's lost is lost, what's won is won.
The guilt has followed me like a stray dog,
The death is like a cloud of black fog.

As my pearly white dress drags along the floor,
The cobbled stone walls glare for ever more.
And before I confess all these thoughts in my head,
To bed, to bed, to bed, to bed!

Henry VIII

Sadie Wood

In 1491,
Henry VII had a son!
Not the heir,
But the spare!

Then in 1502,
The heir bid life adieu,
Leaving Henry the eldest!

He was crowned in 1509,
Due to his blood line.
Crowned Henry VIII
Wealth handed to him on a plate.

He married his brother's widow,
They had a female kiddo
this made Henry sad,
So he pictured Kathryn as bad!

In 1533,
He wedded Anne B,
B for bingo bash or bin?
No, B was for Boleyn

She gave him a princess,
Her name was young Bess,
They proclaimed she loved a different man
So to the tower went young Anne!

Then he married Jane
This marriage didn't end in pain.
She gave birth to Ed,
Then she dropped down dead!

1540 came another wife,
Anne of Cleves was name,
this marriage didn't ruin her life,
She was divorced that year.

Then Miss Howard was 5,
Cathy didn't stay long alive.
For in the next 2 years
She was executed,
What fears!

Then came Miss Parr
The luckiest by far
She outlived Henry

For in '47
He died aged 5x11!

So divorced beheaded his favourite died
Divorced beheaded the last survived

Elements

Sebastian Chapple

Fire is hot,
It can destroy a lot,
It can blow up a whole building!
Its fiery flame,
Can burn up a crane,
Which will make a crash landing!

Ice is cool,
It can freeze a pool,
It likes to have a bit of fun!
Its icy power,
Can shatter a flower,
Though it can be quite troublesome!

Electricity's shocking,
It's totally rocking,
It can power any number of homes!
It can turn on a light,
That can be used in the night,
It can even give energy go drones!

Water is wet,
It can be a big threat,
It can create a gigantic wave!
Whirlpools are sneaky,
Tsunamis are cheeky,
In seconds they can flood a big cave!

Nature is green,
It's a wild dream,
It can tangle you with its spiky weeds!
Green leaves falling,
Willow tree calling,
It can even grow sunflowers from seeds!

Air is swift,
It's as fast as a lift,
It can transform into a giant tornado!
It can control the mist,
To wrap around your fist,
It will be everywhere you go!

The Path by the Wall

Sophie Marshall

Darting along a wall of mud and grass,
A border that separates what we don't know
From here, there is a path. It serves
Hares with twitching noses,
Emerging now and then to
A babble of children running by: while
Men and women stick to the long, dusty road
On which nothing happens,
But the quiet rustling of their shoes,
And what the children say.
The path, coiling like barbed wire,
Oozes on. Forayed and raided by even
The thinnest blade of grass

But the road is houseless,
and leads not to a beach.
To see a hare is rare there
and the eye has but the road.
And the path looks like it goes to some
Fabled place, where women have wanted to go
And be: till, acute, it ends where the wall ends.

Breathe

Annika Nehaniv-Dautenhahn

You don't need to see
To know
Those moments of happiness
To feel
Those hearts you have loved
To hear
The music, the song,
Rewriting our history, all the time
All you need is a heart
Without a heart
You might as well be nothing
A song without words
A book without meaning
To touch, to feel, to hear, to love
To be heard
Can you hear it…
The song of infinity
The time of eternity
That fragile thing they call love

Kerala

Emil Thomas

In the blazing sun
Palaupum wafting around
Home in Kerala

The dog is awake
From the smell of parota
Home in Kerala

In the evening
Family gathering to pray
Home in Kerala

The humid rain falls
The nocturnal creatures hunt
Home in Kerala

Family First

Harvey Denley

To Mummy

She keeps me safe
At night in the dark,
She makes me feel secure,
No matter what,
Because family is first,
She is straightforward,
And open with an honest
Heart she keeps me warm,
And is always caring
Because family is first,
Every night she makes me feel
Cosy and don't forget
Togetherness is key.

An Icy Lament

Jefferson Bird

Stabbing frost
Spine spiking
Unwelcoming, biting and bitter
Unremitting chills
Stone cold agony
Raw and shrivelled skin – a shiver
Agonisingly pierces
Nipping and twinging
Down the spine like an unwelcome critter
Pounding and persistent
An ice cold dagger
Threatening to strike.
It won't cease.
It roams on.

My Best Friend

Jenny Miller

She is a bit weird
She is a bit crazy
And most of the time she is extremely lazy
I haven't known her for long
I have lost friends in the past
You're my best friend forever
So I'll kill you last.

The Desert

Thomas Maguire

Scorching hot yellow
Rubbing smoothly on my toes
Green prickly cacti

I'm from not much to say

Alex Bishop-Court

I'm from not much to say
From a house with a white door
I come from whatever the weather throws our way
From music blaring
The TV flaring
I come from LED wires around my room

Freedom

Cerys Bennison

I write this within my prison – four stark walls that mark the
Borders of my life.
I sense the end descending upon me at last, like an infinite
Russian twilight.
But I shall not fear it.

For my heart, it still soars on in an external dream-dance;
A guardian of the galaxy,
Surfing the hope-studded moonshine with the night dragons,
Frolicking in a golden sunset to the melody of the ocean,
A whistling harmony of secrets.
It flies on the delicate wings of a butterfly, to the land where
Candy tinted cherry blossoms bloom.
Or maybe
It pirouettes with the sylphs of dreamtime, dancing on the
Constellations…………..
Perhaps it will dive into the jade green depths with the mermaids,
Foraging for pearls, or, even fragments of time itself.
Just maybe.
It glides, reaching for the stars, riding upon the chariot to Heaven,
Owning every corner of the world………..

There. My swan song has ended.
At least my sacrifice was not in vain.
I hear them coming again, hopefully for the last time.
But I shall go calmly, knowing my heart still flies on, free .

Where I'm From

Ella O'Shea

I'm from a house with honeycomb walls
a door of overcast sky
a bulb of fireflies hanging near

where a black cat with the pseudonym "Ollie"
writes days
in a house by the car retailer's

I am from a 2 x 1.5 metre room
covered in books, posters and clothes
like a rainbow exploded

I am from a place with music misting round
lingering in the dusty corners
sticking in spiderwebs

I am from a grey city
banked by green rolls of country
A wifi oasis in the middle of Somerset

I am from peaceful pale green and sparky orange
I am from the infinite clouds of knowledge
and the wisps of thought in my head

The Sea

Eloise Edmonds

Some say its waves are pages of a book
holding sea serpents and mermaids
cities lost long ago

some say it is a beast
of churning white waters and jagged rocks
casting sailors and their ships
into its murky depths

some say it's an undiscovered world
full of species never seen by human eye

yet as I stand on the beach
its lapping tide
tickling at my feet
it sings a lonely wailing song
and reveals nothing to me
i smile

Freedom

Kaci James

Freedom is having friends
And not worrying about things

Freedom is having rights
And expressing yourself

Freedom is loving who you wish
And not being afraid
And not worrying

A Moorland Journey

Emilia Birch

The golden grass waved as we passed,
their tips were touched with flame;
and over trampled moorland grass,
the wild horses came.

The bloated sun sat on the hill,
weak rays lit the moor.
Adders crouched under the heather til'
the warm sun coaxed them all.

Stones flew from the road
as we bounced over the pebbles,
the heavens opened and the rain came down
over the drowned black heather.

The storm had gone, the raindrops hung
from arms reached out to catch them.
Dead and gnarled, a dream catcher,
roots and thrayed burnt heather.

Force Majeure

Maddie Mcgowan

Looking from my view, family and friends,
The world working in harmony.

I can give life but take it away just as easily.
The birds fell silent. The animals retreated.

Waiting, waiting, my anticipation is growing strong.

I have arrived.

The banks have burst.

I crave for the attention and the shock of my unannounced arrival.

I engulf everything in my path.

I show no remorse.

I am the tears of nature, spilling forth onto land.
Provoked, goaded, by man's disrespect.

I take no prisoners, no reprimand.
My all consuming power, taking you with me.
Gurgle. Slurp. Guzzle.

I make my escape, leaving misery to cascade.
Devastation and death is my legacy.
I am not a wave. I am a Tsunami, a force to be reckoned with.

A Better World Made by Dreamers

Zainab Ranim

Dream with your heart,
Dream with your soul,
Do not cower from dreams,
But let them fuel you,
Let them lead you to happiness.
You've been given the right to dream,
Use it!
Dreamers will always shine in the darkness,
They will be the sun to guide the happiness out,
Dreamers will be the fire in the darkest hours,
Dreamers will glow,
Dreamers will burn through sadness,
Dreams are the stars in the sky guiding you.
So, look up and be part of the Court of Starlight.

Freedom

Haydn May

is being as free as a gymnast in the middle of a somersault,
as free as a mouse when it finds an abandoned shed,
as free as a hand holding a pen,
as free as a star, shining by itself,
as free as a free radical atom
before it finds another atom.

Unspoken

Emily Yates

Photo of an Afghan girl by Steve McCurry:

Looking at her then,
Her hair is roped up by a cloth and
Her lips pursed and blistered by the sun.
Her eyes, the pupils look so enchanted
By the terror that scared her so badly.
They look red like they've been staring
Right into the burning sky all day.
The green irises are so eye-capturing
Yet the sand has filled them;
The reflection of the mountain implanted in them,
Entwined with the dry weather,
Smudged in with the stunning light.
They're sharp like a knife
And hard like a bullet,
A flare of orange and black
Twisted in their fear.
She looks adrift,
Fearing tomorrow's infinities
And the loss of the past.
With landmines festering,
Bombs going off with intent and intensity.
All they wanted was power,
And all she wanted was mercy.
Nights were unslept
And deaths were unspoken.

Reflection of myself after the Manchester Arena bombing:

Looking at myself in the mirror,
My hair is scraped back
Away from the dark shadows under my eyes,
Black with cold thoughts
And tiredness you can't sleep away.

I hug myself, trying to hold
My cracked pieces together
Before I break,
Everything spilling on the floor.
My eyes are dry from burning tears
And stung red.
I escaped.
But it festers inside me,
Waiting on the edge of my vision,
Waiting to light a spark.
Seeing fires, seeing red,
And dangerous people everywhere.
There could be another one.
My blue irises
Reflect the fear
Which had filled them,
Overflowing with blue tears,
The reflection of that night,
That never goes away.
I feel like I'm looking at someone else's eyes.
I felt like I was looking through someone else's eyes
And running with someone else's body.
Nothing felt real.
"The bang - was it loud?"
People just wanted to know what happened,
Not what's happening to me now.
All they wanted was gossip,
And all I wanted was to be left alone.
There could be another one.
Nights are unslept
And deaths are unspoken.

Every Day When

Kayla Nadienne Putri Bera

I learnt this in the daytime
When I reminded my teacher
To always drink water
And also when my friend and I
Helped a lost ant
Get back to its colony
I learnt this on my birthday
And every visit to Dad's with Mom
Each and every weekend
Then, my sister taught it to me
Through her dead eyed stares
And missing prescription bottles
Behind her locked bedroom door

On a different day
I would learn this lesson at school
As I was figuring out what to become
When I grew up
My friend said
He would be the best crossing guard
To make sure no one got hurt again
On their way to school or back home
And he mentioned our friends
During his speech many times
That earned him an A*
While mine only got a B-

As the sun was at its highest point,
I taught myself this lesson
When I pulled her in close
And whispered only to her
"The world doesn't deserve you
But you deserve the world"
In return she taught me, too
As she joked that she could fit
Her entire world in her hands
And in me telling her
That it simply couldn't be done,

She held my face tenderly
And proved me wrong

It was in the afternoon when
I learnt this lesson from the old man
That I helped cross the street
After he remembered me fondly
As that one student
Who reminded him everyday
To always drink water
He said that I still had
That special sidetracked mind
Which reminded me
To get her those flowers she likes

On a different day,
It would be my friend
Who taught me that lesson
As I had to convince him over the phone
To not let go
No matter what he said
The next day,
I got fired for being late to work
But that friend offered me a better job
I didn't become a crossing guard
But at the very least,
We were able to help people
And make sure no one got hurt again

It was at night
That I began to reminisce
Not only on that lesson,
But also, what I gained from learning it
I wouldn't be complacent today
For I knew many more nights
Await me with more to learn
And this shall be the final lesson
That I teach to my world
For love is not needed for life
But is completely necessary for living

I am Jose Martinez

Khadijah Ahmed

I am Jose Martinez on a perilous journey.
No choice but to part with my hard-earned money,
to those violent gangs who will help me to be someone.
Just like a fairy godmother,
giving life not to a helpless Cinderella,
but to me, a resilient, foolhardy fella.

I am Jose Martinez feeling distressed and distraught.
What about my family?
What happens if I'm caught?
I vision my father and sister working hard all day,
and I cry thinking about my mother, the way she lovingly says Jose.

I am Jose Martinez waiting on the train in the dark.
Waiting for the sound of the vicious dogs' barks.
I lay on the floor wondering whether this will ever finish, whether it will ever be done,
I wait for my fairy godmother, for those gangs with guns.
Please help me godmother for this is my chance, my only chance to start over,
I need your help or I'll live in poverty forever.

I was Jose Martinez, Fairy Godmother took my soul.
She raised her gun and fired an unmerciful blow.
I was thrown off my feet with tears in my eyes,
how can one be so evil, filled with so many lies?
I shut my eyelids and recollect my frightful past,
wondering how many other young men like me won't last.
So Mr. Trump go ahead and build your great wall,
because the world simply chooses to ignore my call.

Darkness Within

O. H.

Everyday I am slowly dying,
Breaking down then start crying.
Rotting from the inside out,
Keeping quiet when I want to scream and shout.
People think that I am fine,
But they don't see my reality all the time.
Stuck in this dark hole,
Getting out was the only goal.
Refusing the drugs that will make me smile,
Even though it's getting harder to keep up this profile.
You feel like your insanity is leaving you,
But you sit, watching not knowing what to do.
Then your mind starts going to dark places,
Get it done quick, easy leave no traces.
But then a voice comes into your mind,
Tears flowing making you blind.
This dark hole is now way too deep,
There is nothing you can do so you lie in a heap.
You don't want to play this game anymore,
Roll the dice and try to find the door.
It comes back for another bite,
Frightened, paralysed in fright.
Now the darkness is suffocating,
All I can do is wait as the demon is slating.
Everyday I was slowly dying,
But then I gave up without trying.

The Last Whale Song

Olivia Hunter

Shells washed up
At the edge of the sunlit reef
Offerings from the tide
And rocks like pointed teeth

Where ships float like petals
Where seagulls fly
And draw arcs in cloud
Across the darkening sky

With the rhythm of sea
Lush green seaweed sways
To mark time that is counted
In number of waves

Atop a sandy bed
The ancient ocean breathes
Near moon-bathing seals
The swirling water seethes

The liquid moonlight
Lapping sand with its tongue
Mimicking a lullaby
Of the last whale song

My Country Nepal
Sid Rai

In the blazing sun
The workers collect the rice
My country Nepal

Burning spices
Fill the streets that I love
My country Nepal

Trapped
Amanda Riney-Lucas

Fly little birdie,
But let me hold your wings,
Be the best,
But let someone else win.
The sky's the limit,
But don't soar too high,
Spread your wings,
But never fly.

Our Latticed Lives

Amelia Peto

The truly free have flown where they please.
Feathered feet follow where the wind has blown
For freedom is fractured, a ceaseless tease.

Dipped wings grace the lake, reflected with ease,
By the light of that luminous dome.
As the truly free have flown where they please

Latticed lives that we lead, this the bird sees
That we scuttle in the brown earth, laid prone.
For freedom is fractured, a ceaseless tease.

If those who fly are free, why do the bees
Always stick close to their honeycombed home?
Haven't they truly flown where they please?

For freedom's a siren's song, sung with ease.
By finding it, we lose it, worked to bone
For freedom is fractured, a ceaseless tease.

But birds leap away, drifting on the breeze
We watch, while we are trapped to bitter stone
As the truly free have flown where they please
For freedom is fractured, a ceaseless tease.

Remnants of the Past

Ani King

Remnants of the past, lingering,
Clinging on to what they know,
Their whispers caught in the wind,
Of yesteryear's tomorrow,

The quietude of the crowd fills the air,
The silence of the bells tolling, long ago,
The stillness of the bustling streets,
Their voices lost in the sorrow,

Soon there is a distant roar,
As the inferno is unleashed,
Screams echo through the walls,
Their spirits now released,

Then it is over,
The massacre complete,

The vestige of the misery that one was,
Fills the heavy air,
A mother embracing a cold, stiff shell,
Muttering a silent prayer.

the dinosaur faces into the east

Charlie Blake

the dinosaur faces into the east
casting a shadow into the sun; standing,
a statue.

his shadow leaves and returns,
the fickle, loyal shadow leaves and returns.

surely as the waves from the beach to the sea and the sea to the beach
surely as the blood to a kill and the washing away of blood by the rain
surely as the wind to the trees and the leaves to the ground
it comes with the sun and leaves with the sun,

and the dinosaur stays ever still,
waiting for his shadow to stay; finding
his place

wishing it was surer than the waves the blood and the trees
and waiting past its end;
till the sun explodes and all worlds go black,
the dinosaur is still and patient.

Darkness in Light

Kevork Milikian

When at break of day
I awoke to a touch,
To a touch of lost memory
At once am running backwards to a familiar obscure horizon
Propelled with an unnatural force
Through a mixture of blinding darkness and muddling bright light
While tussling with grit: trying to get hold to an invisible cord that exists not
I'm shoved, jolted, plunged

And am back where memory star-crossed me like a stuck clock,
Back, to the sound of my name uttered with frightening expectancy;
Shells sound in the background: pleasant sounds, furious gunshots.
And blood and order defying nameless body parts: a bruised sand
Laying on a red-green grass with a over-clouding miasma of black powder;

To the sound of my name, I awoke,
John joggling my feet, jolting me back to sub-consciousness
Run-on, John, I said with every line on my face pleading
Take my shoes and run-on
A furrowed look takes over his face,
The fear of death and the unwillingness to leave me in devil's land;
Take my shoes and run, I said, nodding my head pleadingly.
Rains of gunshot, bitter blood spills all over me, my tongue
As a lifeless body of a loved one, wearing my shoe – drops on me

To a touch, I awoke
It is a fair maiden: tending my wound

A fallen-in-love poem

Megan-Lily Brewster

You sit waiting,
Your heart so close to your mouth you could gag
And then it happens…
The screen lights up and you hungrily feast on the pixels;
He's agreed to go!
…as friends.
You see,
That's the thing about people like him!

When you first noticed him, it was like an explosion in a marvel movie –
POW –
And there you are,
Standing and staring gormlessly at this gorgeous creature -
It's like everything is moving in slow motion…

…Except it's not.
And you can hear the people behind you getting itchy to move (itchy meaning that if you don't move soon they will not hesitate to trample you).

And that's what its like, until you tell them,
And you go… for coffee
…as friends.

But then there's him.
You didn't notice just how unknowingly gorgeous He truly is
Because they're your friend.
You tell them everything.
You couldn't possibly fall for them?

Right?

You sit waiting…
Your heart so close to your mouth you could gag.
And then it happens…

The screen lights up and you hungrily feast on the pixels -
He's agreed to go…
As friends!
You see,
That's what you love about him.

Anguish

Milo Raine-Lower

Secrets;
The protective force field for my woes, wrapped around me so tightly, they leave cavernous wounds. The agony is hidden through smiles and long sleeves; lacerations desperate to be heard but their sound is feeble, not even a whisper as there's a purpose to their silence: safety.

The Real Tale of the Glass Shoe

Ansa Memon

Do we seek beauty? Fellow girls
Please answer me,
We worry about glass ceilings,
Because, how are we meant to break free?

Why do we aim to beautify?
Break bones in order to fly?
Oh so many questions…
But I'm afraid, I haven't much time.

Dear children,
You must see, that
This is free verse
That mirrors my speech.
No sonnet, or villanelle
For I am human and imperfect,
From the skies I had not fell.

Listen closely,
One child reached above
And pulled down something pretty,
But instead of trading;
It was utilised.

Upon her feet,
A crystal-like glaze,
That drew everyone's attention,
And would lower their gaze,

You know the story,
Such events occur
That only one shoe remains,
But that is where this tale should have ended.

We've come to a point,
Where our fears have reached a peak;
But, a ceiling made with only half the materials,
Is weak.

Break it!

A Choice
Hannah De Meo

▷A CHOICE◁

[redacted] we are [redacted] rooted
[redacted] in [redacted] nations [redacted]
[redacted] that are [redacted] willing to
sacrifice [redacted] fellow [redacted]
[redacted] human s[redacted]

This pulling in my gut is not just a weight
it is a mechanism;
cement and elastic, all coated
in a fine layer of dust
For it has not been lifted for years now.

Is this where anger stems from?
Thrust down raw throats and left undigested?

[redacted] let this be [redacted]
[redacted] our [redacted] fight [redacted]
[redacted] for [redacted]
[redacted] the world, [redacted]

If we are to embrace the opportunities of the future and overcome the present dangers together, there can be no substantive for strong, sovereign, and independent nations, nations that are rooted in the histories and invested in their destiny, nations that seek allies to befriend, not enemies to conquer, and most important of all, nations that are home to men and women who are willing to sacrifice for their countries, their fellow citizens, and for all that is best in the human spirit.

This is the ancient wish of every people and the deepest yearning that lives inside every sacred soul. So let this be our mission, and let this be our message to the world. We will fight together, sacrifice together, and stand together for peace, for freedom, for justice, for family, for humanity, and for the almighty God who made us all. Thank you, God bless you, God bless the nations of the world, and God bless the United States of America. Thank you very much.

The birch in my street; the twig I knew

Owoh Ugonna Alexander

Embedded with flimsy Shaw,
It's the birch I saw, it dwelled in my street.

Growing chiefly on dry gravel soils.
Bearing twigs so slender and reddish brown,
Becoming dull chalky white with age.

Its winter buds, a smooch of fluff, so brown and
Red. Its leaves, triangular in shape,

Its fruits; shimmering to my throat,
Consisting of wing nutlets.

It is the birch in my street, it danced with the winds,
Sang with the Nightingales,

It owned a twig, so light and floppy, brassy and cheeky.

When the birch swayed with the winds,
It lumbered with sturdiness, refusing to sway.

It is the twig I knew. It pleaded the Toco toucans for liberty.

"Please friends, use your long beaks to crouch me
Out, I don't want to belong".

The Toco toucans affixed in pardon sheer their twig friend.

It is the twig I knew, it tugged in happiness
As it stuffed to the ground dancing for freedom founds it.

Poem analysis:
The birch symbolizes the British
The twigs symbolizes the British colonies and Eire
The stubborn twig was Nigeria, trying to found independence.
The Toco toucans were the Nigeria elites who struggled for freedom

Being There

Romany Whittall

I always kept an umbrella
At the bottom of my school-bag
Right-hand side, close up against my back
Bright patterns pressed together, plastic wings curled up tight
Protective, but ready to take flight
At any moment

This day has stuck with me, though:
Got halfway to the gate
Before I noticed
There was no plastic handle
Nudging my back with each step

Checked

No umbrella

Looked up at the sky
Cerulean blue, cloudless, bright
Continued, forwards
No hesitation

However,
On leaving the school later
The sky turned evil
Invaded by menacing, pacing, roaring clouds
That threw torrents of water over everything
I was soaked instantly
Cold seeped into my skin
Clothes drenched; shoes saturated
Squelching, shivering, stuttering into every step
Hair waterlogged and dripping down my neck
Skin chafed raw by shirt and trousers
Fingers and feet void of feeling
The longest journey home ever
Onwards, onwards

Finally, I staggered through the door
Met by my father, bearing a towel
Who half-lectured me as I dried myself off
Saying I needed the protection
Should have brought a shield
Should have gone back for it

But I know
If I had gone to retrieve it
It would never have needed to rescue me

My Darling at War

Vaishnavi Shandilya

Strokes of rouge ignite flames,
Willowy wisps of ebony billow,
Barren, weather-beaten, blackened windows to the soul,
Bloody crimson blooms on ashen ivory,
Cluttering yet permeating silences resound and reverberate,
My love at War…

Obsidian clouds cast heavy inflamed shadows,
Speck of copper stain the black-brown,
Lightning bolts of pasty white line the once ebony,
Poppies adorn the onyx rows,
Heavy atmosphere pressures cries to the dirt,
My Darling at War.

Fell Winterland

Afra Sterne-Rodgers

The aged boughs of birch shift in the wind,
Disturbing the dusting of white resting
So gently on their supple fingertips.
Dormice turn their tails and flee to their homes
As the Ice of Winter falls once again.
The wind casts nets of frost and revelry
Over the tors and moors of its domain.
The ponds and lakes and rivers do entrap
The poor unwitting residents therein
Who must do no other but wait in vain
For the fine day in which the sun reclaims
The patronage of this fell Winterland.
The swallow, restless, flees his frosted home
He knows the barbarous winter is come.

The Walk Home

Alayna Ismail

I find myself sandwiched
between two layers of grey:
A murky, dismal sky overhead,
And a pedestrian slab of concrete beneath me.
Such bleakness could make a journey feel obsolete,
But occasionally, something just slips through.
Be it a fleck of fauna growing through the pavement,
Or a speck of sunlight peering through the clouds,
Providing spatters of light to my surroundings.
But most colourful of all are the people,
With their unusual gaits
And milling children
And peculiar conversations
Snippets of which can just be deciphered
If one listens closely enough
As I often do to embellish my walk home.
Where I find myself sandwiched between two layers of grey,
And discover everything in between.

Burn

Bethany Martin

Verb – to cause or be destroyed by fire

It was a pleasure to burn
They had her believe
The feeling was freedom they said
Then they started to steal away at her skin
And let her cry out to the waterless world –
Hurled into darkness, alone,
Half dead.
So, as her cheeks tinged red,
As she held her head high,
As she whispered and whimpered
And wasted and cried,
She tried to believe she was fine;
After all she was blessed to be alive.

Then they poured on gasoline,
She breathed in and remained –
For the luxury of burning,
The luxury of pain
Or maybe just for their will
and maybe just their gain
Maybe just for their delight.

"Some have no heat, no light"
They reminded
So burning was a pleasure –
All should be so like minded
And take the gift with grace.
Her heart raced but they just paced the floor.
The flames licked higher at her heels
And tore at her tears
But she stared with no feeling
Wheels of thought simply wrecking her brain,
Now revealing that what she'd been told
Was a lie.

Her fears went against her privilege –
She was supposed to be too lucky to be in pain
But still she hurt, still she cried.

She should learn to just cope, not be small
Her thoughts called
It's a pleasure to burn after all.
They had told her she should want the flames that scalded her
They had told her the warmth and the light was to be prided
And treasured for all of her life.

They had lied,
she decided.

It was a pleasure to burn,
They'd had her believe
They'd said she'd enjoy it when she'd questioned,
They'd said she'd be freed from fear by the flames,
They'd said she be happy,
They'd left out the pain,
They'd said to want more than just burning was greed
For nothing but personal gain.

They said she was hopeless without flames.

She said they should all go to hell,
It's a pleasure to burn after all.

Beautiful Youths

Charlotte Lee

Look, young children, at the sky above,
The stars that are more ancient than earth itself.
You are looking at what our ancestors have seen, with the same love
That fills your eyes and self.
Look at Orion, the hunter and archer,
My guiding light, my brave marcher.

Look around you, boys and girls, at the land that rolls away.
You tread the same road millions have walked before,
But your journey will be different, come what may,
And you will see what your ancestors saw.
Build on that world of mystery,
And our friends of the past won't just be history.

Look far out at the horizon, the next time you go to the coast,
And know that it was our ancestors that traversed the water,
And discovered that the world was not flat, and of their exploits they could boast,
For they had built on knowledge for their son and daughter.
Thank them, remember them, and learn again,
For they would be proud if you could add to the knowledge they found then.

Look at one another, beautiful youths,
And hold one another's hands in joy,
And listen to a voice that soothes;
Hold on dearly to your toy,
And remember these happy days,
These peaceful ways.

Look around, innocent eyes,
There is a wonderful world to find.
Never lose hope, nor give into lies;
Our ancestors have built a bold world for us.
Be brave, dear children, beautiful youths, innocent eyes,
There is a wonderful future beyond, and with the sun you will rise.

Aurora

Jonah Carter

Rolling, whirling, twisting, turning,
My breath pours out like smoke from a fire.
I take in my surroundings, slowly learning,
Of this icy utopia that I admire.

A place where the snow falls upon the petals of a flower,
A place where my hands grow numb by the hour,
A place where the sky's countless colours are put on display,
A place where you stand in awe, nothing to do, nothing to say,
But watch.

Watch how time slips off the edge of reality.
Watch how the slumbering mountains reside undisturbed.
Watch how the trees sway, swivel and swing to the tune of
tranquillity.
Watch how silence patrols through the night unperturbed,
Hushing the distant howling of civilisation,
A land of turbulence, indignation.

Breathing, smiling, feeling, living,
I stand liberated.
No such thing existed, more sublime to see.
No such place existed, I'd rather be.
No such time existed, where happiness had returned to me;
I stand intoxicated.
For nature's beverage of beauty – a wondrous wine –
Was gifted the gods' heavenly nectar, tasting euphoric as ever, sweet
and divine.

Moonlit Dreamer

Isobel Sophia Kavanagh

Upon our dancing duo,
We're a syncopated beat.
You complete the rests and rhythms
That you know I fail to reach.

With you comes the sun's light
On the darkest of my days.
Your words a sweet elixir,
Each an emblem of its rays.

You glance at me, among the crowd
I beam at your beautiful face.
But to others I'm a wandering fool
Who's staring into space.

It's no more than a flicker,
You smile and to me hope is brought
But around us Judgement seethes,
So with others you'll consort.

That is until you think of me,
Of you I do the same.
We'll meet and laugh until we drop.
This buoyant, blissful game!

It's easier away from here,
With just us two alone,
Unspoken of, our late night chats
That parents won't condone.

You murmur and you mutter
From a distant midnight dream.
Unsleeping, but at peace I am,
A devoted, selfless scheme.

So far away you are from me,
A land of cloud and moon,
Yet in my arms you greet the dawn
Two starlit, snoozing spoons.

But though you say you love me,
And you'll be there come what may
From you I crave a different love,
To which your heart cannot give way.

And so as winter turns to spring,
It's time we turned the page,
Will our chapters cope uniquely?
In cruel time, I'll have to gauge.

And so that crowd of hundreds,
Will conceal you from my view
Our days together over
And a broken heart's debut.

The Sakura Tree

Chanice Barrow-Francis

There it was, standing in the middle, beauty at its finest.
Its petals as soft as cotton wool.
Its scent was as fresh as cut grass on a summer's morning.
As the wind howled bitterly, nature departed from its bundle of cotton candy.
Like a ballerina, the petals twirled elegantly in the air before hitting the ground.
Who would have thought that a tree could bring such joy and warmth?
Twig that was once bare and bleak, was now smothered in blossoms.
Not a stone could be seen on the pathway among the floral sheets.
As I looked intently at creation, I was pleased to be in the season where Sakura trees blossom.

Cape and Cowl

Laura Rodrigues Silva

Clara. The best superhero name.
Two mentors with two protégés.
He couldn't help but be the prodigal son.
She couldn't help but raise the gun.

Love. Seems all too real
so give her time to heal.
The pain hits too close to home.
She's better off all alone.

Letters. Endless pages.
Time travel back to the stone ages.
Falling down the rabbit hole
anywhere to get her away from her own soul.

An armor, made with unwanted feelings.
It's peeling, revealing,
the Hatter living in her mind.

A hero. A tragic hero.
Putting her mask on so no one sees
the cracks in the costume she wears to please.

LIVE CANON